1 sauce, 50 dishes

Linda Doeser

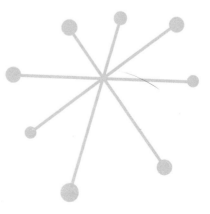

First published in 2011
LOVE FOOD is an imprint of Parragon Books Ltd

Parragon
Queen Street House
4 Queen Street
Bath BA1 1HE, UK

ISBN: 978-1-4454-0640-4

Printed in Indonesia

Written by Linda Doeser
Photography by Mike Cooper
Home economy by Lincoln Jefferson

Notes for the Reader
This book uses both metric and imperial measurements. Follow
the same units of measurement throughout; do not mix metric and
imperial. All spoon measurements are level: teaspoons are assumed
to be 5 ml, and tablespoons are assumed to be 15 ml. Unless
otherwise stated, milk is assumed to be full fat, eggs and individual
vegetables are medium, and pepper is freshly ground black pepper.

The times given are an approximate guide only. Preparation times
differ according to the techniques used by different people and the
cooking times may also vary from those given. Optional ingredients,
variations or serving suggestions have not been included in the
calculations.

Recipes using raw or very lightly cooked eggs should be avoided
by infants, the elderly, pregnant women, convalescents and anyone
suffering from an illness. Pregnant and breastfeeding women are
advised to avoid eating peanuts and peanut products. Sufferers
from nut allergies should be aware that some of the ready-made
ingredients used in the recipes in this book may contain nuts.
Always check the packaging before use.

Contents

Introduction

A well-made, tasty sauce is often the secret that turns a good dish into a great one – and there are few sauces that are more versatile and more popular than tomato sauce. It makes a great accompaniment to plainly cooked meat, poultry, fish, vegetables and eggs, and works superbly well as the basis for braised dishes, stews and layered bakes. It's the perfect topping for pasta, essential for classic pizzas and makes a delicious hot or cold dipping sauce for all kinds of vegetables and fritters.

A simple tomato sauce is quick and easy to make. There's no risk of curdling and it doesn't require much attention while it simmers. It can be made in advance and reheated, the ingredients are inexpensive and readily available and it keeps well in the refrigerator and freezer. All the dishes in this book can be made with just the basic sauce – and will be truly delicious – but the recipes also include a huge number of variations. Tomatoes go so well with other ingredients – from chillies to mushrooms and from ginger to olives – that the options are almost endless. There are substantial versions that include bacon, cheese, beans or other vegetables; spicy sauces with warm Middle Eastern flavours, hot Mexican chillies, subtle Indian mixes or a savoury barbecue tang; rich sauces with cream, butter and wine; and piquant mixtures with olives, capers, oranges, horseradish, anchovies or apples.

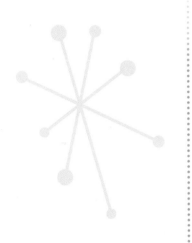

Basic Tomato Sauce Ingredients

Tomatoes are, of course, the main and most important ingredient in a basic tomato sauce and there is debate about whether fresh or canned tomatoes make the best sauce. Fresh tomatoes that have ripened fully in the sun are sweet and full of flavour – particularly if they're home grown – and will almost certainly make a really tasty sauce. However, out-of-season tomatoes that have to be imported may have been picked before they are ripe and are often watery and tasteless. Good-quality canned tomatoes are available all year round and are excellent for making tomato sauce. In blind tastings, many people have either been unable to taste any difference between the same sauce made with fresh and canned tomatoes or have actually preferred the one made with canned.

Plum tomatoes, whether fresh or canned, are perfect for cooking as they have denser, less watery flesh than round tomatoes. Many round tomato varieties are selected by suppliers because they are robust enough to withstand the rigours of transportation rather than for their flavour, although recent years have seen an increase in the range of tomatoes available. Cherry tomatoes tend to be more expensive but are usually sweet and fragrant. Never use unripe tomatoes for making tomato sauce as no amount of added sugar will counteract their acidity and sharpness – keep them for making chutney. However, you can use varieties that turn yellow when ripe, but the sauce may be less visually appealing than when made with red tomatoes.

Tomato purée intensifies the flavour of tomatoes and is particularly useful if you are using fresh tomatoes that may not have been sun-ripened. Sugar helps to counteract the acidity of tomatoes, some of which can be very sharp. A useful tip when you don't have any tomato purée is to omit the sugar and add 1–2 tablespoons of tomato ketchup instead.

Various members of the onion family add flavour and emphasis to tomato sauce. The common brown onion is a good all-rounder and can be used in any recipe but some recipes work even better with other varieties. Sweet onions include red onions, which have reddish-purple skins and pink-tinged flesh, and Spanish onions, which are very large and mild with a mellow flavour. Shallots are much smaller than most varieties of onion and are elongated in shape. They are far less astringent than onions, although they do vary in strength and have a distinctive taste that is not quite onion and not quite garlic. Spring onions, with a white bulb and leafy green tops, are mild and cook quickly. Garlic is a natural partner for tomatoes and gives extra depth to the flavour of the sauce. The number of cloves to include is a matter of personal taste. If you are not very keen on the flavour, add a whole clove when softening the onion and then remove and discard it before adding the other ingredients. This will give just a hint of garlic that you won't find overwhelming.

Most recipes in this book recommend using olive oil, which not only has a rich flavour and aroma that complement tomatoes but is also a healthy choice as it contains monounsaturated fat. It just seems to go perfectly with the flavour of tomatoes and is the natural choice for Mediterranean and Middle Eastern recipes. You do not need to use expensive extra virgin oil – keep that for salad dressings. Virgin oil, from the second pressing, is perfect for cooking, but avoid olive oils simply labelled 'pure' as they have often been heat-treated and consequently have lost all flavour. If you're using other vegetable oils, perhaps because the sauce is very spicy, choose one with a bland flavour, such as sunflower, safflower, groundnut or corn oil.

As a rule, fresh herbs are always more flavoursome than dried, although both bay leaves and oregano are often used dried. Basil is the tomato herb as it complements the flavour superbly. The

leaves are easily bruised so it is often better to tear it by hand rather than to chop it with a knife. Both curly and flat-leaf parsley and fresh coriander are also good choices. One or two bay leaves add a distinctive flavour and aroma to robust tomato sauces but don't forget to remove them before serving.

The final ingredient in the basic tomato sauce is celery, which provides extra flavour and texture. If you dislike the 'strings' in celery, they can be removed easily by running a vegetable peeler along the length of the stick.

Preparing Fresh Tomatoes

To peel tomatoes, cut a cross in the top of the tomatoes and put them into a heatproof bowl. Pour in boiling water to cover and leave to stand for 1 minute. Drain and peel off the skins with a sharp knife; they should slip off easily. Don't try to peel more than 4–5 tomatoes at one time or some will begin to cook in the boiling water.

If you have a gas cooker, you can also peel tomatoes by skewering them, one at a time, with a metal fork, holding them in the gas flame and turning for 1–2 minutes, until the skin splits and wrinkles. Leave to cool, then pull off the skins with your fingers.

Always cut out the top part of the tomato where the stem grew and the central pale core, which is quite hard and inedible, using a sharp knife.

Most recipes in this book do not suggest deseeding tomatoes, but a few do. There are also recipes where the finished sauce should be pressed through a sieve. This removes the seeds as well as the vegetables and other solid matter.

To deseed tomatoes, cut them in half with a sharp knife, then scoop out the seeds using a teaspoon.

Basic Tomato Sauce

Makes about 600 ml/1 pint

* 25 g/1 oz butter
* 2 tbsp olive or other vegetable oil
* 1 onion, finely chopped
* 1 garlic clove, finely chopped
* 1 celery stick, finely chopped
* 400 g/14 oz canned chopped tomatoes or 500 g/
   1 lb 2 oz plum tomatoes, peeled, cored and chopped
* 2 tbsp tomato purée
* brown sugar, to taste
* 1 tbsp chopped fresh herbs and/or 1–2 tsp dried herbs
   and/or 1–2 bay leaves
* 100 ml/3½ fl oz water
* salt and pepper

Melt the butter with the oil in a saucepan. Add the onion, garlic and celery and cook over a low heat, stirring occasionally, for 5 minutes, until softened. Stir in the tomatoes, tomato purée, sugar to taste, the herbs and water and season to taste with salt and pepper. Increase the heat to medium and bring to the boil, then reduce the heat and simmer, stirring occasionally, for 15–20 minutes, until thickened.

This is the basic recipe that all 50 dishes in this book are based on. For each recipe these ingredients are highlighted (*) for easy reference. Please note that quantities may vary so please check these carefully.

Easy

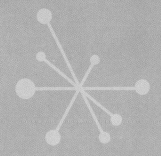

Barbecued Beef Kebabs

1. First, make the sauce. Melt the butter with the oil in a saucepan. Add the Spanish onion, garlic and celery and cook over a low heat, stirring occasionally, for 5 minutes, until softened. Add the chillies and cook, stirring occasionally, for a further 3 minutes. Stir in the tomatoes, tomato purée, mustard powder, bay leaf, Worcestershire sauce, honey and vinegar and season to taste with salt and pepper. Increase the heat to medium and bring to the boil, then reduce the heat and simmer, stirring occasionally, for 15–20 minutes, until thickened.

2. Remove the pan from the heat and leave to cool slightly. Remove and discard the bay leaf, then transfer the sauce to a food processor or blender and process until smooth. Press the sauce through a sieve into a bowl.

3. Preheat the barbecue or grill. Brush four metal skewers with oil. Cut each red onion into eight wedges. Trim the spring onions and cut in half widthways. Thread the steak cubes onto the skewers, alternating them with onion wedges and spring onion halves.

4. Transfer about three quarters of the sauce to a sauceboat. Brush half the remainder over the kebabs and cook over hot coals or under the preheated grill, turning frequently and brushing with the remaining sauce from the bowl, for 8–10 minutes, until the meat is cooked to your liking. Serve immediately with the reserved sauce.

Serves 4

olive oil, for brushing
2 red onions
4 spring onions
700 g/1 lb 9 oz rump steak, cut into cubes

Barbecue sauce
※ 25 g/1 oz butter
※ 2 tbsp olive oil
1 Spanish onion, finely chopped
※ 2 garlic cloves, finely chopped
※ 1 celery stick, finely chopped
1–2 fresh red chillies, deseeded and chopped
※ 400 g/14 oz canned chopped tomatoes
※ 2 tbsp tomato purée
1 tsp mustard powder
※ 1 bay leaf
2 tbsp Worcestershire sauce
3 tbsp clear honey
1 tbsp red wine vinegar
※ salt and pepper

White Beans with Prosciutto & Tomato Sauce

1. Put the beans into a large saucepan, pour in water to cover and bring to the boil over a medium–high heat. Reduce the heat and simmer for 45 minutes, until the beans are just tender. Drain well and set aside.

2. Melt the butter with the oil in a saucepan. Add the onions, garlic and celery and cook over a low heat, stirring occasionally, for 5 minutes, until softened. Stir in the tomatoes, tomato purée, sugar to taste, basil, prosciutto and water and season to taste with salt and pepper. Increase the heat to medium and bring to the boil.

3. Add the beans, reduce the heat and simmer, stirring occasionally, for 30 minutes. Transfer to a warmed serving dish and serve immediately.

Serves 4–6

500 g/1 lb 2 oz dried haricot beans, soaked overnight and drained

✳ 55 g/2 oz butter

✳ 4 tbsp olive oil

✳ 2 onions, finely chopped

✳ 2 garlic cloves, finely chopped

✳ 2 celery sticks, finely chopped

✳ 800 g/1 lb 12 oz canned chopped tomatoes

✳ 2 tbsp tomato purée

✳ brown sugar, to taste

✳ 1 tbsp chopped fresh basil

115 g/4 oz prosciutto, chopped

✳ 100 ml/3½ fl oz water

✳ salt and pepper

Italian-style Gammon

1. First, make the sauce. Melt the butter with the oil in a saucepan. Add the shallots, garlic and celery and cook over a low heat, stirring occasionally, for 5 minutes, until softened. Stir in the tomatoes, tomato purée, sugar to taste, parsley and wine and season to taste with salt and pepper. Increase the heat to medium and bring to the boil, then reduce the heat and simmer, stirring occasionally, for 15–20 minutes, until thickened.

2. Meanwhile, preheat the grill. Bring a large saucepan of lightly salted water to the boil. Add the pasta, bring back to the boil and cook for 8–10 minutes, until tender but still firm to the bite. Rub the gammon steaks with the sage and cook under the preheated grill for 6–7 minutes on each side, until tender and cooked through.

3. Drain the pasta, tip into a warmed serving dish and toss with the butter. Put the gammon steaks on top and pour the tomato sauce over them. Sprinkle with the olives and serve immediately.

Serves 4

225 g/8 oz dried tagliatelle verde

4 thick gammon steaks

1 tsp dried sage

25 g/1 oz butter

8 black olives, stoned and halved

salt

Tomato sauce

* 25 g/1 oz butter
* 2 tbsp olive oil
  2 shallots, finely chopped
* 2 garlic cloves, finely chopped
* 1 celery stick, finely chopped
* 400 g/14 oz canned chopped tomatoes
* 2 tbsp tomato purée
* brown sugar, to taste
* 1 tbsp chopped fresh flat-leaf parsley
  100 ml/3½ fl oz dry white wine
* salt and pepper

Lamb in Tomato Sauce

1. Melt the butter in a large saucepan. Add the lamb and cook over a medium heat, stirring frequently, for 6–8 minutes, until evenly browned. Stir in the garlic, 125 ml/4 fl oz of the wine and all the stock, season to taste with salt and pepper and bring to the boil. Reduce the heat and simmer, stirring occasionally, for 30 minutes, until the lamb is tender.

2. Meanwhile, make the sauce. Melt the butter with the oil in a saucepan. Add the shallots, garlic and celery and cook over a low heat, stirring occasionally, for 5 minutes, until softened. Stir in the tomatoes, tomato purée, sugar to taste, parsley and water and season to taste with salt and pepper. Increase the heat to medium and bring to the boil, then reduce the heat and simmer, stirring occasionally, for 15–20 minutes, until thickened.

3. Mix the flour to a paste with the remaining wine in a small bowl, then stir into the lamb mixture. Cook, stirring constantly, for 3 minutes, or until the cooking liquid has thickened. Stir in the tomato sauce.

4. Transfer the stew to a warmed serving dish, garnish with parsley and serve immediately.

Serves 4

55 g/2 oz butter

1 kg/2 lb 4 oz boned shoulder of lamb, trimmed and cut into 4-cm/1½-inch cubes

1 garlic clove, finely chopped

150 ml/5 fl oz dry white wine

225 ml/8 fl oz chicken stock

1 tbsp plain flour

salt and pepper

Tomato sauce

25 g/1 oz butter

2 tbsp olive oil

2 shallots, finely chopped

2 garlic cloves, finely chopped

1 celery stick, finely chopped

400 g/14 oz canned chopped tomatoes

2 tbsp tomato purée

brown sugar, to taste

2 tbsp chopped fresh flat-leaf parsley, plus extra to garnish

100 ml/3½ fl oz water

salt and pepper

Chicken Croquettes in Rich Tomato Sauce

① Heat half the oil in a saucepan. Add the onion and celery and cook over a low heat, stirring occasionally, for 5 minutes, until softened. Add the chicken, tomatoes and potatoes and cook, stirring frequently, for 8–10 minutes. Transfer the mixture to a food processor and process until smooth. Scrape into a bowl and leave to cool, then chill for 1 hour.

② Meanwhile, make the sauce. Remove the bacon rind and dice the bacon. Melt the butter with the bacon rind in a saucepan. Add the bacon, shallot, garlic, celery and carrot and cook over a low heat, stirring occasionally, for 5 minutes. Stir in the tomatoes and cook, stirring occasionally, for 5 minutes. Stir the cornflour into the stock and pour it into the pan. Season to taste with salt and pepper. Cover and simmer, stirring occasionally, for 20 minutes, until thickened. Remove and discard the bacon rind.

③ Lightly dust your hands with flour and divide the chicken mixture into 8–12 pieces. Roll each into a small croquette. Place the eggs in a shallow bowl and spread out the breadcrumbs in a separate shallow bowl. Dip the croquettes into the beaten egg, then into the breadcrumbs to coat.

④ Heat the remaining oil in a frying pan. Add the croquettes and cook over a medium heat, turning once, for 10 minutes. Drain on kitchen paper. Pour the sauce over the croquettes, sprinkle with the parsley and serve immediately.

Serves 4

6 tbsp olive oil
1 onion, finely chopped
1 celery stick, finely chopped
225 g/8 oz cooked chicken, finely chopped
3 tomatoes, peeled and finely chopped
550 g/1 lb 4 oz boiled potatoes, finely chopped
plain flour, for dusting
2 eggs, lightly beaten
115 g/4 oz dry breadcrumbs
1 tbsp chopped fresh parsley

Rich tomato sauce
1 rasher lean bacon
✳ 25 g/1 oz butter
✳ 1 shallot, finely chopped
✳ 1 garlic clove, finely chopped
✳ 1 celery stick, finely chopped
1 carrot, finely chopped
✳ 400 g/14 oz canned chopped tomatoes
2 tsp cornflour
300 ml/10 fl oz chicken stock
✳ salt and pepper

Sole with Tomato Sauce

1. First, make the sauce. Melt the butter with the oil in a saucepan. Add the onion, garlic and celery and cook over a low heat, stirring occasionally, for 5 minutes, until softened. Stir in the tomatoes, tomato purée, sugar to taste, parsley and water and season to taste with salt and pepper. Increase the heat to medium and bring to the boil, then reduce the heat and simmer, stirring occasionally, for 20 minutes, until thickened.

2. Meanwhile, preheat the oven to 180°C/350°F/Gas Mark 4. Trim the sides of the fish fillets to make them straight, reserving the trimmings, then cut them in half lengthways. Season to taste with salt and pepper and sprinkle with the lemon juice.

3. Lightly beat the ricotta in a bowl with a fork until smooth. Chop the fish trimmings and stir them into the ricotta with the Tabasco. Spread the mixture over the strips of fish and roll up. Put the rolls into an ovenproof dish, seam-side down, in a single layer. Pour the stock over them and bake in the preheated oven for 20 minutes, until the fish flakes easily.

4. Using a slotted spoon, carefully transfer the fish rolls to a warmed serving dish. Spoon the tomato sauce over them and sprinkle over the olives and gherkin. Serve immediately.

Serves 4

4 large sole fillets, skinned
2 tbsp lemon juice
55 g/2 oz ricotta cheese
dash of Tabasco sauce
300 ml/10 fl oz fish stock
4 black olives, stoned and halved
1 pickled gherkin, chopped
salt and pepper

Tomato sauce
* 25 g/1 oz butter
* 2 tbsp olive oil
* 1 onion, finely chopped
* 2 garlic cloves, finely chopped
* 1 celery stick, finely chopped
* 400 g/14 oz canned chopped tomatoes
* 2 tbsp tomato purée
* brown sugar, to taste
* 1 tbsp chopped fresh flat-leaf parsley
* 100 ml/3½ fl oz water
* salt and pepper

Prawns & Feta in Tomato Sauce

1. First, make the sauce. Melt the butter with the oil in a saucepan. Add the onion, garlic and celery and cook over a low heat, stirring occasionally, for 5 minutes, until softened. Stir in the tomatoes, tomato purée, sugar to taste, herbs and water. Increase the heat to medium and bring to the boil, then reduce the heat and simmer, stirring occasionally, for 15 minutes.

2. Stir in the wine and season to taste with salt and pepper. Increase the heat and bring back to the boil, then reduce the heat and simmer, stirring occasionally, for a further 30 minutes, until thickened.

3. Stir in the prawns and feta cheese and cook, stirring frequently, for 5–8 minutes, until the prawns are cooked and the cheese has melted. Remove and discard the bay leaf. Transfer to a warmed serving dish and serve immediately.

Serves 4

500 g/1 lb 2 oz raw tiger prawns, peeled and deveined

85 g/3 oz feta cheese, crumbled

Tomato sauce
* 25 g/1 oz butter
* 2 tbsp olive oil
* 1 onion, finely chopped
* 3 garlic cloves, finely chopped
* 1 celery stick, finely chopped
* 1 kg/2 lb 4 oz plum tomatoes, peeled, cored and chopped
* 2 tbsp tomato purée
* brown sugar, to taste
* 1 tbsp chopped fresh flat-leaf parsley
* 1 fresh basil sprig, chopped
* 1 bay leaf
* ½ tsp dried oregano
* 100 ml/3½ fl oz water
  225 ml/8 fl oz dry white wine
* salt and pepper

Tomato Soup

1. Melt the butter with the oil in a saucepan. Add the onion, garlic and celery and cook over a low heat, stirring occasionally, for 5 minutes, until softened. Stir in the tomatoes, tomato purée and water. Increase the heat to medium and bring to the boil, then reduce the heat and simmer, stirring occasionally, for 10 minutes.

2. Increase the heat to medium, then stir in sugar to taste, the basil and stock. Season to taste with salt and pepper. Bring to the boil, then reduce the heat and simmer for a further 10 minutes.

3. Taste and adjust the seasoning, adding salt and pepper if needed. Ladle into warmed bowls, garnish with basil and serve immediately.

Serves 4

* 25 g/1 oz butter
* 2 tbsp olive oil
* 1 large onion, finely chopped
* 2 garlic cloves, finely chopped
* 1 celery stick, finely chopped
* 500 g/1 lb 2 oz plum tomatoes, peeled, cored and chopped
* 2 tbsp tomato purée
* 100 ml/3½ fl oz water
* brown sugar, to taste
* 1 tbsp chopped fresh basil, plus extra to garnish
* 300 ml/10 fl oz vegetable stock
* salt and pepper

Penne in Tomato Sauce with Two Cheeses

① First, make the sauce. Melt the butter with the oil in a saucepan. Add the shallots, garlic and celery and cook over a low heat, stirring occasionally, for 5 minutes, until softened. Stir in the tomatoes, tomato purée, sugar to taste, oregano and water and season to taste with salt and pepper. Increase the heat to medium and bring to the boil, then reduce the heat and simmer, stirring occasionally, for 15–20 minutes, until thickened.

② Meanwhile, bring a large saucepan of lightly salted water to the boil. Add the pasta, bring back to the boil and cook for 8–10 minutes, until tender but still firm to the bite. Drain and return to the pan.

③ Add the tomato sauce and the cheeses to the pasta and toss well over a very low heat until the cheeses have melted. Transfer to a warmed serving dish and serve immediately.

Serves 4

450 g/1 lb dried penne

115 g/4 oz Bel Paese cheese, diced

55 g/2 oz Parmesan cheese, grated

salt

Tomato sauce

* 25 g/1 oz butter
* 2 tbsp olive oil
* 2 shallots, finely chopped
* 2 garlic cloves, finely chopped
* 1 celery stick, finely chopped
* 400 g/14 oz canned chopped tomatoes
* 2 tbsp tomato purée
* brown sugar, to taste
* 1 tsp dried oregano
* 100 ml/3½ fl oz water
* salt and pepper

Courgette, Pepper & Tomato Gratin

1. Melt the butter with the oil in a large saucepan. Add the onion, garlic, celery, courgettes and peppers and cook over a low heat, stirring occasionally, for 5 minutes, until softened. Stir in the tomatoes, tomato purée, sugar to taste, basil, bay leaf and water and season to taste with salt and pepper. Increase the heat to medium and bring to the boil, then reduce the heat and simmer, stirring occasionally, for 30 minutes, until thickened and the vegetables are tender.

2. Meanwhile, preheat the grill. Remove and discard the bay leaf and spoon the vegetable mixture into a flameproof dish. Sprinkle with the anchovies and Parmesan and cook under the preheated grill for 3–5 minutes, until the top is golden brown and bubbling. Serve immediately.

Serves 4

* 25 g/1 oz butter
* 2 tbsp olive oil
* 1 onion, thinly sliced
* 2 garlic cloves, finely chopped
* 1 celery stick, finely chopped
  700 g/1 lb 9 oz courgettes, sliced
  2 large red peppers, deseeded and sliced
* 400 g/14 oz canned chopped tomatoes
* 2 tbsp tomato purée
* brown sugar, to taste
* 1 tbsp chopped fresh basil
* 1 bay leaf
* 100 ml/3½ fl oz water
  6 canned anchovy fillets, drained and chopped
  55 g/2 oz Parmesan cheese, grated
* salt and pepper

Favourite

Lasagne

1. Heat the oil in a large saucepan. Add the pancetta and cook over a medium heat, stirring occasionally, for 2–3 minutes. Reduce the heat to low, add the garlic and onion and cook, stirring occasionally, for 5 minutes, until softened.

2. Add the beef, increase the heat to medium and cook, stirring frequently and breaking it up with the spoon, for 8–10 minutes, until evenly browned. Stir in the carrots, celery and mushrooms and cook, stirring occasionally, for a further 5 minutes. Add the oregano, pour in the wine and stock and stir in the sun-dried tomato paste. Season to taste with salt and pepper. Bring to the boil, reduce the heat and simmer for 40 minutes.

3. Meanwhile, preheat the oven to 190°C/375°F/Gas Mark 5. Make alternating layers of the beef sauce, lasagne sheets and Parmesan in a large, rectangular ovenproof dish. Pour the tomato sauce over the top to cover completely. Bake in the preheated oven for 30 minutes. Remove the dish from the oven and leave to stand for 10 minutes, then cut into squares and serve with a mixed salad.

Serves 4

2 tbsp olive oil

55 g/2 oz pancetta or bacon, chopped

1 garlic clove, finely chopped

1 onion, chopped

225 g/8 oz fresh beef mince

2 carrots, chopped

2 celery sticks, chopped

115 g/4 oz mushrooms, chopped

pinch of dried oregano

5 tbsp red wine

150 ml/5 fl oz beef stock

1 tbsp sun-dried tomato paste

225 g/8 oz dried no-precook lasagne sheets

115 g/4 oz Parmesan cheese, grated

✳ 1 quantity Basic Tomato Sauce (see page 8)

salt and pepper

mixed salad, to serve

Spaghetti & Meatballs in Tomato Sauce

1. Tear the bread into pieces and place into a large bowl. Pour over the milk and leave to soak for 5 minutes. Add the beef, garlic, breadcrumbs, 5 tablespoons of the Parmesan, the egg, lemon rind and thyme. Season to taste with salt and pepper, then mix well with your hands until thoroughly combined. Shape the mixture into about 30 walnut-sized balls and put them on a baking sheet. Chill in the refrigerator for 30 minutes.

2. Meanwhile, pour the tomato sauce into a large saucepan and place over a low heat. Heat gently until warmed through.

3. Melt 115 g/4 oz of the butter in a frying pan. Add the meatballs, in batches, and cook over a medium heat, turning occasionally, for 6–8 minutes, until evenly browned. Using a slotted spoon, transfer the meatballs to the tomato sauce. When they have all been added, cover the pan and simmer for 25–30 minutes, until cooked through.

4. Meanwhile, bring a large pan of salted water to the boil. Add the spaghetti, bring back to the boil and cook for 8–10 minutes, until tender but still firm to the bite. Drain, tip into a warmed serving dish and toss with the remaining butter. Spoon the meatballs on top and pour the sauce over them. Sprinkle with the remaining Parmesan and serve immediately.

Serves 4

2 thick slices bread, crusts removed

3 tbsp milk

1 kg/2 lb 4 oz fresh beef mince

3 garlic cloves, finely chopped

25 g/1 oz dry breadcrumbs

85 g/3 oz Parmesan cheese

1 egg, lightly beaten

2 tsp grated lemon rind

1 tsp dried thyme

1 quantity Basic Tomato Sauce (see page 8)

150 g/5½ oz butter

500 g/1 lb 2 oz dried spaghetti

salt and pepper

Hawaiian Pizza

1. To make the pizza dough, sift the flour and salt into a bowl and stir in the yeast. Make a well in the centre and pour in the oil and lukewarm water, then mix to a soft dough. Turn out onto a lightly floured surface and knead for 10 minutes, until smooth and elastic. Shape into a ball, put it into an oiled plastic bag and leave to rise in a warm place for about 1 hour, until doubled in volume.

2. Melt the butter with the oil in a saucepan. Add the onion and celery and cook over a low heat, stirring occasionally, for 5 minutes, until softened. Stir in the tomatoes, tomato purée, sugar to taste, oregano and water and season to taste with salt and pepper. Increase the heat to medium and bring to the boil, then reduce the heat and simmer, stirring occasionally, for 15–20 minutes, until thickened. Remove from the heat and set aside.

3. Preheat the oven to 220°C/425°F/Gas Mark 7. Brush a baking sheet with oil. Knock back the dough and knead briefly on a lightly floured surface. Roll out into a round and transfer to the prepared baking sheet. Push up a rim all the way around.

4. Spread the tomato sauce evenly over the pizza base. Sprinkle evenly with the ham and pineapple, then top with the cheese. Drizzle with oil and bake in the preheated oven for 15–20 minutes, until crisp and golden. Serve immediately.

Serves 2

- 15 g/½ oz butter
- 1 tbsp olive oil, plus extra for brushing and drizzling
- 1 small onion, finely chopped
- ½ celery stick, finely chopped
- 200 g/7 oz canned chopped tomatoes
- 1 tbsp tomato purée
- brown sugar, to taste
- ½ tsp dried oregano
- 3 tbsp water
- 175 g/6 oz ham, diced
- 225 g/8 oz canned pineapple chunks in juice, drained
- 55 g/2 oz Cheddar cheese, grated
- salt and pepper

Pizza dough
- 225 g/8 oz strong white flour, plus extra for dusting
- 1 tsp salt
- ½ tsp easy-blend dried yeast
- 1 tbsp olive oil
- 150 ml/5 fl oz lukewarm water

Gammon Steaks with Tomato & Sage Sauce

1. First, make the sauce. Melt the butter with the oil in a saucepan. Add the onions, garlic, celery and green pepper and cook over a low heat, stirring occasionally, for 5 minutes, until softened. Stir in the tomatoes, tomato purée, sugar to taste, fresh sage and water and season to taste with salt and pepper. Increase the heat to medium and bring to the boil, then reduce the heat and simmer, stirring occasionally, for 25–30 minutes, until thickened.

2. Preheat the grill. Rub the gammon steaks with the dried sage and season to taste with pepper. Cook under the preheated grill for 5 minutes on each side, until tender and cooked through. Transfer to warmed serving plates, spoon the sauce over them and serve immediately.

Serves 4

4 gammon steaks
1 tsp dried sage
pepper

Tomato & sage sauce
* 25 g/1 oz butter
* 2 tbsp olive oil
* 2 large onions, thinly sliced
* 2 garlic cloves, finely chopped
* 1 celery stick, finely chopped
  1 green pepper, deseeded and cut into julienne strips
* 800 g/1 lb 12 oz canned chopped tomatoes
* 3 tbsp tomato purée
* brown sugar, to taste
* 1 tbsp chopped fresh sage
* 100 ml/3½ fl oz water
* salt and pepper

Barbecued Chicken

1. First, make the sauce. Melt the butter with the oil in a saucepan. Add the onion, garlic, celery and ginger and cook over a low heat, stirring occasionally, for 5 minutes, until softened. Stir in the tomatoes, tomato purée, Worcestershire sauce, vinegar, lemon juice, sugar, oregano, bay leaf, nutmeg and water and season to taste with salt and pepper. Increase the heat to medium and bring to the boil, then reduce the heat and simmer, stirring occasionally, for 30–40 minutes, until thickened.

2. Meanwhile, preheat the barbecue or grill. Brush the skin sides of the chicken halves with half the oil and put them skin-side down on the barbecue grill or skin-side uppermost on the grill rack. Cook over hot coals or under the preheated grill for 10 minutes, then brush with the remaining oil, turn them over and cook for a further 20 minutes, until golden brown.

3. Brush the chicken with half the sauce. Continue to cook, turning and brushing frequently with the remaining sauce, for 15–20 minutes, until cooked through and tender. Transfer to a warmed serving dish and serve immediately.

Serves 4

2 double poussins or spring chickens, about 900 g/ 2 lb each, cut in half

4 tbsp olive oil

Barbecue sauce
- 25 g/1 oz butter
- 2 tbsp olive oil
- 1 onion, finely chopped
- 2 garlic cloves, finely chopped
- 1 celery stick, finely chopped
- 1-cm/½-inch piece fresh ginger, finely chopped
- 400 g/14 oz canned chopped tomatoes
- 2 tbsp tomato purée
- 1 tbsp Worcestershire sauce
- 2 tbsp red wine vinegar
- 2 tbsp lemon juice
- 1 tbsp brown sugar
- 1 tsp dried oregano
- 1 bay leaf
- pinch of grated nutmeg
- 2 tbsp water
- salt and pepper

Turkey Escalopes with Tomato & Apple Sauce

1. First, make the sauce. Melt the butter with the olive oil in a saucepan. Add the shallots and apple and cook over a low heat, stirring occasionally, for 5 minutes, until softened. Stir in the tomatoes, tomato purée, sugar to taste, nutmeg and water and season to taste with salt and pepper. Increase the heat to medium and bring to the boil, then reduce the heat and simmer, stirring occasionally, for 15–20 minutes, until thickened. Remove the sauce from the heat and leave to cool slightly.

2. Put the turkey between two sheets of clingfilm and beat with a meat mallet or the side of a rolling pin until thin and even. Put the flour into a shallow dish and season to taste with salt and pepper. Lightly beat the egg in a separate shallow dish and spread out the breadcrumbs in a third shallow dish.

3. Dip the escalopes, one at a time, first in the flour, then in the egg and, finally, in the breadcrumbs to coat. Melt the butter with the sunflower oil in a large frying pan. Add the escalopes, in batches, and cook over a medium heat for 1 minute on each side, until golden brown. Reduce the heat and cook for a further 3–4 minutes on each side, until tender.

4. Meanwhile, gently reheat the sauce. Transfer the escalopes to warmed serving plates and pour the sauce over them. Garnish with parsley and serve immediately.

Serves 4

4 turkey escalopes
3 tbsp plain flour
1 egg
55 g/2 oz dry breadcrumbs
55 g/2 oz butter
2 tbsp sunflower oil
salt and pepper
chopped fresh flat-leaf parsley,
  to garnish

Tomato & apple sauce
25 g/1 oz butter
2 tbsp olive oil
2 shallots, finely chopped
1 eating apple, peeled, cored
  and diced
400 g/14 oz canned chopped
  tomatoes
2 tbsp tomato purée
brown sugar, to taste
pinch of grated nutmeg
100 ml/3½ fl oz water
salt and pepper

17

Crab Cakes with Rich Tomato Sauce

1. Peel both kinds of potatoes and cut into chunks. Cook in a large saucepan of salted boiling water for 15–20 minutes, until tender but not falling apart. Drain well, return to the pan and mash roughly, then leave to cool.

2. Stir the egg into the cooled potatoes, then stir in the crabmeat, flour, mustard powder and tarragon. Season to taste with salt and pepper. Lightly flour your hands, scoop up 2 tablespoons of the mixture and shape into a cake. Repeat, flouring your hands as required, until all the mixture has been used up. Put the crab cakes on a baking sheet and chill in the refrigerator for 30 minutes to firm up.

3. Meanwhile, make the sauce. Melt the butter with 2 tablespoons of oil from the jar of sun-dried tomatoes in a saucepan. Add the shallots, garlic and celery and cook over a low heat, stirring occasionally, for 5 minutes, until softened. Stir in the fresh tomatoes, sun-dried tomatoes, sun-dried tomato paste, sugar to taste, wine and tarragon. Season to taste with salt and pepper. Increase the heat to medium and bring to the boil, then reduce the heat and simmer, stirring occasionally, for 15–20 minutes, until thickened.

4. Heat the sunflower oil in a large frying pan. Add the crab cakes, in batches, and cook for 2–3 minutes on each side, until golden brown and heated through. Serve immediately with the sauce and lemon wedges for squeezing over.

Serves 4

225 g/8 oz potatoes
450 g/1 lb sweet potatoes
1 egg, lightly beaten
280 g/10 oz white crabmeat
2 tbsp plain flour, plus extra for dusting
1 tbsp mustard powder
2 tsp chopped fresh tarragon
4 tbsp sunflower oil
salt and pepper
lemon wedges, to serve

Rich tomato sauce
25 g/1 oz butter
4 sun-dried tomatoes in oil, drained and chopped
2 shallots, finely chopped
2 garlic cloves, finely chopped
1 celery stick, finely chopped
500 g/1 lb 2 oz plum tomatoes, peeled, cored and chopped
2 tbsp sun-dried tomato paste
brown sugar, to taste
100 ml/3½ fl oz dry white wine
1 tbsp chopped fresh tarragon
salt and pepper

Margherita Pizza

1. Melt the butter with the oil in a saucepan. Add the onion, garlic and celery and cook over a low heat, stirring occasionally, for 5 minutes, until softened. Stir in the canned tomatoes, tomato purée, sugar to taste, chopped basil and water and season to taste with salt and pepper. Increase the heat to medium and bring to the boil, then reduce the heat and simmer, stirring occasionally, for 15–20 minutes, until thickened. Remove from the heat and set aside.

2. Preheat the oven to 220°C/425°F/Gas Mark 7. Brush a baking sheet with oil. Knock back the dough and knead briefly on a lightly floured surface. Roll out into a round and transfer to the prepared baking sheet. Push up a rim all the way around.

3. Spread the tomato sauce evenly over the base. Arrange the mozzarella and tomato slices alternately on top. Coarsely tear the basil leaves and put them on the pizza, then sprinkle with the Parmesan. Drizzle with oil and bake in the preheated oven for 15–20 minutes, until crisp and golden. Serve immediately.

Serves 2

- 15 g/½ oz butter
- 1 tbsp olive oil, plus extra for brushing and drizzling
- 1 small onion, finely chopped
- 1 garlic clove, finely chopped
- ½ celery stick, finely chopped
- 200 g/7 oz canned chopped tomatoes
- 1 tbsp tomato purée
- brown sugar, to taste
- 1 tbsp chopped fresh basil
- 3 tbsp water
- 1 quantity Pizza Dough (see page 38)
- plain flour, for dusting
- 140 g/5 oz mozzarella cheese, sliced
- 4 tomatoes, sliced
- 1 fresh basil sprig
- 2 tbsp grated Parmesan cheese
- salt and pepper

19

Fettuccine with Tomato & Mushroom Sauce

1. First, make the sauce. Melt the butter with the oil in a saucepan. Add the onion, garlic and celery and cook over a low heat, stirring occasionally, for 5 minutes, until softened. Stir in the tomatoes, tomato purée, wine and mushrooms. Increase the heat to medium and bring to the boil, then reduce the heat and simmer, stirring occasionally, for 15–20 minutes, until thickened.

2. Meanwhile, bring a large saucepan of lightly salted water to the boil. Add the fettuccine, bring back to the boil and cook for 8–10 minutes, until tender but still firm to the bite. Drain, tip into a warmed serving dish and toss with the butter.

3. Stir sugar to taste and the basil into the sauce and season to taste with salt and pepper. Pour the sauce over the pasta, toss well and sprinkle with the Parmesan. Serve immediately.

Serves 4

450 g/1 lb dried fettuccine
15 g/½ oz butter
2 tbsp grated Parmesan cheese
salt

Tomato & mushroom sauce
* 25 g/1 oz butter
* 2 tbsp olive oil
* 1 large onion, finely chopped
* 2 garlic cloves, finely chopped
* 1 celery stick, finely chopped
* 400 g/14 oz canned chopped tomatoes
* 2 tbsp tomato purée
  4 tbsp dry red wine
  115 g/4 oz mushrooms, sliced
* brown sugar, to taste
* 1 tbsp chopped fresh basil
* salt and pepper

20

Special Macaroni Cheese

① First, make the sauce. Melt the butter with the oil in a saucepan. Add the onion, garlic and celery and cook over a low heat, stirring occasionally, for 5 minutes, until softened. Stir in the tomatoes, tomato purée, sugar to taste, basil and water and season to taste with salt and pepper. Increase the heat to medium and bring to the boil, then reduce the heat and simmer, stirring occasionally, for 15–20 minutes, until thickened.

② Meanwhile, preheat the oven to 190°C/375°F/Gas Mark 5. Grease an ovenproof dish with butter. Bring a large saucepan of lightly salted water to the boil. Add the macaroni, bring back to the boil and cook for 8–10 minutes, until tender but still firm to the bite. Drain well.

③ Mix together the Parmesan and Gruyère in a bowl. Spoon one third of the tomato sauce into the prepared dish, cover with one third of the macaroni and sprinkle with one third of the mixed cheeses. Repeat twice. Mix together the breadcrumbs and the basil and sprinkle over the top. Dot with the butter and bake in the preheated oven for 20–25 minutes, until the topping is golden brown. Serve immediately.

Serves 4

225 g/8 oz dried macaroni

115 g/4 oz Parmesan cheese, grated

175 g/6 oz Gruyère cheese, grated

25 g/1 oz fresh breadcrumbs

1 tbsp chopped fresh basil

15 g/½ oz butter, plus extra for greasing

salt

Tomato sauce

✳ 25 g/1 oz butter

✳ 2 tbsp olive oil

✳ 1 small onion, finely chopped

✳ 2 garlic cloves, finely chopped

✳ 1 celery stick, finely chopped

✳ 400 g/14 oz canned chopped tomatoes

✳ 2 tbsp tomato purée

✳ brown sugar, to taste

✳ 1 tbsp chopped fresh basil

✳ 100 ml/3½ fl oz water

✳ salt and pepper

Spicy

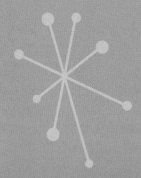

Beef Enchiladas in Piquant Tomato Sauce

① Heat the corn oil in a frying pan. Add the onion and chillies and cook over a low heat, stirring occasionally, for 5 minutes. Add the beef, increase the heat to medium and cook, stirring frequently and breaking it up with the spoon, for 8–10 minutes, until evenly browned. Remove the pan from the heat and stir in half the cheese.

② To make the sauce, melt the butter with the olive oil in a saucepan. Add the onion, garlic and chilli and cook over a low heat, stirring occasionally, for 5–8 minutes, until the onion is golden brown. Stir in the tomatoes, tomato purée, sugar to taste, oregano and cayenne pepper and season to taste with salt and pepper. Increase the heat to medium and bring to the boil. Reduce the heat, stir in the cream and simmer, stirring occasionally, for 15–20 minutes, until thickened. Remove from the heat and leave to cool slightly.

③ Meanwhile, preheat the oven to 180°C/350°F/Gas Mark 4. Heat a frying pan and brush with corn oil. One at a time, dip the tortillas in the sauce, shake off any excess and cook in the frying pan for 30 seconds on each side. Transfer to a large plate, put a tablespoon of the meat mixture in the centre and roll up. Put the filled tortillas, seam-side down, in a large ovenproof dish and pour the remaining sauce over them. Sprinkle with the remaining cheese and bake in the preheated oven for 15–20 minutes. Garnish with coriander and serve immediately.

Serves 6

1 tbsp corn oil, plus extra for brushing

1 onion, finely chopped

2 fresh green chillies, deseeded and chopped

280 g/10 oz fresh beef mince

115 g/4 oz Cheddar cheese, grated

18 tortillas

chopped fresh coriander, to garnish

Piquant tomato sauce
* 25 g/1 oz butter
* 2 tbsp olive oil
* 1 onion, finely chopped
* 2 garlic cloves, finely chopped
  1 fresh green chilli, deseeded and chopped
* 400 g/14 oz canned chopped tomatoes
* 2 tbsp tomato purée
* brown sugar, to taste
* 1 tsp dried oregano
  ½ tsp cayenne pepper
  125 ml/4 fl oz double cream
* salt and pepper

Steak with Tomato & Horseradish Sauce

1. First, make the sauce. Melt the butter with the oil in a saucepan. Add the onion, garlic and celery and cook over a low heat, stirring occasionally, for 5 minutes, until softened. Stir in the tomatoes, tomato purée, horseradish, parsley and water and season to taste with salt and pepper. Increase the heat to medium and bring to the boil, then reduce the heat and simmer, stirring occasionally, for 15–20 minutes, until thickened.

2. Meanwhile, preheat the grill to high. Brush the steaks with oil and season to taste with salt and pepper.

3. Cook the steaks under the preheated grill for 2–3 minutes on each side for rare or 3–4 minutes on each side for medium. For well-done steaks, cook for 3 minutes on each side, then reduce the heat and grill for a further 5 minutes on each side. Transfer to warmed plates, spoon the sauce over them and serve immediately.

Serves 6

6 sirloin steaks, about 225 g/ 8 oz each
olive oil, for brushing
salt and pepper

Tomato & horseradish sauce
* 25 g/1 oz butter
* 2 tbsp olive oil
* 1 onion, finely chopped
* 2 garlic cloves, finely chopped
* 1 celery stick, finely chopped
* 400 g/14 oz canned chopped tomatoes
* 2 tbsp tomato purée
  2 tbsp creamed horseradish
* 2 tbsp chopped fresh flat-leaf parsley
* 100 ml/3½ fl oz water
* salt and pepper

Pork Chops Mexican Style

1. Rub the pork chops all over with the cut sides of the garlic. Put them on a plate, cover with clingfilm and chill in the refrigerator for 4 hours.

2. Meanwhile, make the sauce. Melt the butter with the olive oil in a saucepan. Add the onion, garlic and celery and cook over a low heat, stirring occasionally, for 5 minutes, until softened. Stir in the tomatoes, tomato purée, sugar to taste, chillies and water and season to taste with salt and pepper. Increase the heat to medium and bring to the boil, then reduce the heat and simmer, stirring occasionally, for 20 minutes. Remove from the heat and leave to cool slightly, then transfer to a food processor or blender and process to a purée.

3. Heat the corn oil in a large frying pan. Add the pork chops and cook over a medium heat for 5 minutes on each side, until evenly browned. Pour in the sauce, reduce the heat, cover and simmer, turning the chops once or twice, for 15–20 minutes, until cooked through and tender.

4. Meanwhile, peel, stone and slice the avocado, then sprinkle with the lime juice to prevent discoloration. When the chops are ready, transfer to a warmed serving dish, pour the sauce over them and top with the avocado. Serve immediately.

Serves 4

4 pork chops
2 garlic cloves, halved
2 tbsp corn oil
1 avocado
2 tbsp lime juice

Tomato & chilli sauce
25 g/1 oz butter
2 tbsp olive oil
1 onion, finely chopped
2 garlic cloves, finely chopped
1 celery stick, finely chopped
650 g/1 lb 7 oz plum tomatoes, peeled, cored and chopped
2 tbsp tomato purée
brown sugar, to taste
3 fresh green chillies, deseeded and finely chopped
300 ml/10 fl oz water
salt and pepper

24

Lamb Steaks with Sweet & Spicy Tomato Sauce

1. First, make the sauce. Melt the butter with the oil in a saucepan. Add the shallots, garlic, celery and red pepper and cook over a low heat, stirring occasionally, for 5 minutes, until softened. Stir in the tomatoes, tomato purée, mustard, honey, sugar, chilli flakes, cayenne pepper, paprika and water and season to taste with salt and pepper. Increase the heat to medium and bring to the boil, then reduce the heat and simmer, stirring occasionally, for 15–20 minutes, until thickened.

2. Preheat the grill or barbecue. Brush the lamb steaks with oil and cook under the preheated grill or over hot coals for 3–5 minutes on each side, depending on how well done you like them. Transfer to serving plates and spoon over the sauce. Garnish with basil and serve immediately.

Serves 6

6 lamb steaks
olive oil, for brushing
chopped fresh basil, to garnish

Sweet & spicy tomato sauce
* 25 g/1 oz butter
* 2 tbsp olive oil
2 shallots, finely chopped
* 2 garlic cloves, finely chopped
* 1 celery stick, finely chopped
1 red pepper, deseeded and chopped
* 500 g/1 lb 2 oz plum tomatoes, peeled, cored and chopped
* 2 tbsp tomato purée
2 tbsp Dijon mustard
1 tbsp clear honey
* 2 tbsp brown sugar
1 tbsp chilli flakes
1 tbsp cayenne pepper
1 tbsp paprika
* 100 ml/3½ fl oz water
* salt and pepper

Easy Chicken Curry

1. Melt the butter with half the oil in a saucepan. Add the onion, garlic, ginger, chilli and celery and cook over a low heat, stirring occasionally, for 5 minutes, until softened. Stir in the tomatoes, tomato purée, sugar to taste, spices and water and season to taste with salt and pepper. Increase the heat to medium and bring to the boil, then reduce the heat and simmer, stirring occasionally, for 15–20 minutes, until thickened.

2. Meanwhile, heat the remaining oil in a frying pan. Add the chicken and cook over a medium heat, stirring frequently, for 5–7 minutes, until lightly browned all over. Remove with a slotted spoon.

3. Stir the chicken and cream into the sauce and simmer for 6 minutes, until the meat is tender and cooked through. Add the spinach and cook, stirring constantly, for 2–4 minutes, until wilted. Bring back to the boil, then transfer to a warmed serving dish. Serve immediately with naan bread.

Serves 4

- 25 g/1 oz butter
- 4 tbsp olive oil
- 1 onion, finely chopped
- 2 garlic cloves, finely chopped
- 1 tbsp chopped fresh ginger
- 1 fresh green chilli, deseeded and chopped
- 1 celery stick, finely chopped
- 400 g/14 oz canned chopped tomatoes
- 2 tbsp tomato purée
- brown sugar, to taste
- ½ tsp ground cumin
- ½ tsp ground coriander
- ½ tsp ground turmeric
- ¼ tsp garam masala
- 100 ml/3½ fl oz water
- 600 g/1 lb 5 oz diced chicken
- 150 ml/5 fl oz double cream
- 200 g/7 oz baby spinach
- salt and pepper
- warm naan bread, to serve

26

Chicken with Tomato & Cinnamon Sauce

1. Melt the butter with the oil in a flameproof casserole. Season the chicken well with salt and pepper, add to the casserole and cook over a medium heat, turning frequently, for 8–10 minutes, until evenly browned. Remove from the casserole and set aside.

2. Add the onion, garlic and celery to the casserole and cook over a low heat, stirring occasionally, for 5 minutes, until softened. Stir in the tomatoes, tomato purée, mustard, sugar to taste, lemon juice, stock, oregano and cinnamon and season to taste with salt and pepper. Increase the heat to medium and bring to the boil, then reduce the heat and simmer, stirring occasionally, for 15 minutes, until thickened.

3. Return the chicken to the casserole and spoon the sauce over it. Cover and simmer, stirring occasionally, for 30 minutes, until the chicken is tender and cooked through. Serve immediately.

Serves 4

- 55 g/2 oz butter
- 2 tbsp olive oil
- 4 chicken quarters
- 1 onion, finely chopped
- 2 garlic cloves, finely chopped
- 1 celery stick, finely chopped
- 400 g/14 oz canned chopped tomatoes
- 2 tbsp tomato purée
- 1 tsp Dijon mustard
- brown sugar, to taste
- 2 tbsp lemon juice
- 3 tbsp chicken stock
- 1 tsp dried oregano
- ¾ tsp ground cinnamon
- salt and pepper

27

Red Snapper in Hot Pepper & Tomato Sauce

1. First, make the sauce. Heat the oil in a saucepan, then add the onion, garlic, celery and chilli and cook over a low heat, stirring occasionally, for 5 minutes, until softened. Stir in the pimientos, tomatoes, tomato purée, sugar to taste, coriander, olives and water and season to taste with salt and pepper. Increase the heat to medium and bring to the boil, then reduce the heat and simmer, stirring occasionally, for 15–20 minutes, until thickened.

2. Meanwhile, preheat the oven to 180°C/350°F/Gas Mark 4. Mix together the flour, chilli powder, salt and pepper in a plastic bag. Add the fish fillets, a few at a time, hold the top closed and shake gently to coat. Heat the oil in a frying pan, then add the fish, in batches, and cook for 5 minutes on each side, until golden brown. Transfer the fish to a large ovenproof dish and set aside.

3. Halve the eggs, remove the yolks and chop. (You do not need the whites.)

4. Pour the sauce over the fish and bake in the preheated oven for 10–15 minutes, until the flesh flakes easily. Sprinkle with the chopped egg yolks. Garnish with coriander and serve immediately.

Serves 4

55 g/2 oz plain flour
1 tsp chilli powder
1 tsp salt
1 tsp pepper
900 g/2 lb red snapper fillets
3 tbsp olive oil
2 hard-boiled eggs

Hot pepper & tomato sauce
* 2 tbsp olive oil
* 1 onion, finely chopped
* 2 garlic cloves, finely chopped
* 1 celery stick, finely chopped
  1 fresh red chilli, deseeded and finely chopped
  115 g/4 oz drained pimientos, finely chopped
* 400 g/14 oz canned chopped tomatoes
* 2 tbsp tomato purée
* brown sugar, to taste
* 1 tbsp chopped fresh coriander, plus extra to garnish
  55 g/2 oz pimiento-stuffed olives, sliced
* 100 ml/3½ fl oz water
* salt and pepper

28

West African Spicy Prawns

1. First, make the sauce. Melt the butter with the oil in a saucepan. Add the onion and garlic and cook over a low heat, stirring occasionally, for 5 minutes, until softened. Stir in the tomatoes, tomato purée, sugar to taste, oregano, bay leaf and water and season to taste with salt and pepper. Increase the heat to medium and bring to the boil, then reduce the heat and simmer, stirring occasionally, for 20–25 minutes, until thickened.

2. Meanwhile, heat the oil in a large frying pan. Add the onions and garlic and cook over a low heat, stirring occasionally, for 5 minutes, until softened. Add the prawns and cook, stirring constantly, for 5 minutes, then add the ham and cook, stirring constantly, for a further 5 minutes.

3. Stir the thyme, basil and cayenne pepper into the prawn mixture, add the bay leaf and season to taste with salt and pepper. Remove the tomato sauce from the heat and strain it into the prawn mixture. Simmer, stirring frequently, for 15 minutes. Remove and discard the bay leaf. Transfer to a warmed serving dish and serve immediately.

Serves 4

125 ml/4 fl oz olive oil

2 onions, finely chopped

1 garlic clove, finely chopped

350 g/12 oz raw prawns, peeled and deveined

225 g/8 oz ham, diced

1 tsp chopped fresh thyme

1 tsp chopped fresh basil

½ tsp cayenne pepper

1 bay leaf

salt and pepper

Tomato sauce

* 25 g/1 oz butter
* 2 tbsp olive oil
* 1 small onion, finely chopped
* 2 garlic cloves, finely chopped
* 500 g/1 lb 2 oz plum tomatoes, peeled, cored and chopped
* 2 tbsp tomato purée
* brown sugar, to taste
* 1 tsp dried oregano
* 1 bay leaf
* 100 ml/3½ fl oz water
* salt and pepper

Potato Wedges with Chilli Tomato Sauce

1. First, make the sauce. Melt the butter with the oil in a saucepan. Add the onion, garlic and celery and cook over a low heat, stirring occasionally, for 5 minutes, until softened. Stir in the tomatoes, tomato purée, chillies, vinegar, sugar to taste and water and season to taste with salt and pepper. Increase the heat to medium and bring to the boil, then reduce the heat and simmer, stirring occasionally, for 20–30 minutes, until thickened.

2. Meanwhile, preheat the oven to 240°C/475°F/Gas Mark 9. Brush a roasting tin with 2 tablespoons of the oil and put it in the oven to heat. Cut the potatoes in half and then into wedges. Brush the potato wedges with the remaining oil.

3. Remove the roasting tin from the oven and spread out the potato wedges in a single layer in the base. Sprinkle with the paprika and sea salt to taste. Roast in the preheated oven, turning occasionally, for 20–30 minutes, until golden brown and crisp all over.

4. Stir the coriander into the sauce and spoon into a serving bowl. Transfer the potato wedges to a warmed serving dish and serve immediately with the sauce.

Serves 4

150 ml/5 fl oz olive oil
4 baking potatoes
1 tbsp sweet paprika
sea salt

Chilli tomato sauce
* 25 g/1 oz butter
* 2 tbsp olive oil
* 1 onion, finely chopped
* 2 garlic cloves, finely chopped
* 1 celery stick, finely chopped
* 400 g/14 oz canned chopped tomatoes
* 2 tbsp tomato purée
  2–3 fresh red chillies, deseeded and finely chopped
  2 tbsp red wine vinegar
* brown sugar, to taste
* 100 ml/3½ fl oz water
* 1 tbsp chopped fresh coriander
* salt and pepper

Courgette Fritters with Peppery Tomato Sauce

① First, make the sauce. Melt the butter with the oil in a saucepan. Add the shallots, garlic, celery and cloves and cook over a low heat, stirring occasionally, for 5 minutes, until softened. Remove and discard the garlic and cloves. Add the breadcrumbs and cook, stirring frequently, for 3 minutes. Stir in the tomatoes, tomato purée, sugar to taste and water. Increase the heat to medium and bring to the boil, then reduce the heat and simmer, stirring occasionally, for 30 minutes, until thickened.

② Meanwhile, coarsely grate the courgettes onto a clean tea towel, then gather up the sides and squeeze tightly to remove the excess moisture. Transfer the courgettes to a bowl, stir in the cheese, eggs and flour and season to taste with salt and pepper.

③ Pour the groundnut oil into a large frying pan to a depth of 2 cm/¾ inch and heat. Add three heaps of the courgette mixture, each 2 tablespoonfuls, flatten slightly and cook for 2–3 minutes on each side. Remove and drain on kitchen paper. Keep warm while you cook more fritters in the same way until all the mixture has been used.

④ Transfer the fritters to a warmed serving plate. Remove the sauce from the heat and season lightly with salt and very generously with pepper and transfer to a warmed serving bowl. Serve immediately.

Serves 4–6

500 g/1 lb 2 oz courgettes
55 g/2 oz Parmesan cheese, grated
2 eggs, lightly beaten
4 tbsp plain flour
groundnut oil, for deep-frying
salt and pepper

Peppery tomato sauce
25 g/1 oz butter
2 tbsp olive oil
2 shallots, finely chopped
2 garlic cloves
1 celery stick, finely chopped
2 cloves
3 tbsp dry breadcrumbs
400 g/14 oz canned chopped tomatoes
2 tbsp tomato purée
brown sugar, to taste
100 ml/3½ fl oz water
salt and pepper

Comforting

Steak with Sweet & Sour Tomato Relish

① First, make the relish. Melt the butter with the olive oil in a saucepan. Add the shallot, garlic and celery and cook over a low heat, stirring occasionally, for 5 minutes, until softened. Stir in the cherry tomatoes, tomato purée, sugar, vinegar, ginger and lime and season to taste with salt and pepper. Increase the heat to medium and bring to the boil, then reduce the heat and simmer, stirring occasionally, for 30 minutes, until thickened. Remove the pan from the heat, transfer the relish to a bowl, cover with clingfilm and leave to cool.

② Meanwhile, using a sharp knife, cut through each steak horizontally almost completely to make a pocket. Spread 1 teaspoon of the creamed horseradish in each pocket. Rub the steaks with the garlic and season well with salt and pepper. Put them on a plate, cover with clingfilm and leave to stand for 30 minutes.

③ Preheat the grill. Brush the steaks with sunflower oil and cook under the preheated grill for 2–3 minutes on each side for medium-rare. If you prefer your steak well done, reduce the heat and grill for a further 5–8 minutes on each side. Serve immediately with the relish.

Serves 4

4 sirloin steaks, about 225 g/
    8 oz each
4 tsp creamed horseradish
2 garlic cloves, finely chopped
sunflower oil, for brushing
salt and pepper

Sweet & sour tomato relish
※ 15 g/½ oz butter
※ 1 tbsp olive oil
1 shallot, finely chopped
※ 1 garlic clove, finely chopped
※ ½ celery stick, finely chopped
※ 250 g/9 oz cherry tomatoes
※ 1 tbsp tomato purée
※ 55 g/2 oz brown sugar
50 ml/2 fl oz white wine
    vinegar
1 piece stem ginger (from a
    jar), drained and chopped
½ lime, thinly sliced
※ salt and pepper

Prosciutto & Blue Cheese Parcels with Buttery Tomato Sauce

1. First, make the sauce. Melt 25 g/1 oz of the butter in a saucepan. Add the shallots, garlic and celery and cook over a low heat, stirring occasionally, for 5 minutes, until softened. Stir in the tomatoes, tomato purée, sugar to taste and wine and season to taste with salt and pepper. Increase the heat to medium and bring to the boil, then reduce the heat and simmer, stirring occasionally, for 15–20 minutes, until thickened.

2. Meanwhile, lay a slice of prosciutto on a board and put a second slice across it to form a cross. Put one quarter of the cheese in the centre, sprinkle with 1 teaspoon of the chives and add one quarter of the diced pear. Sprinkle with one quarter of the walnuts and fold over the sides of the prosciutto to make a parcel. Make three more parcels in the same way. Preheat the grill.

3. Dice the remaining butter. Remove the pan from the heat and beat the sauce well, then beat in the butter, one piece at a time, making sure that each piece has been fully incorporated before adding the next. Stir in the chives and basil and reheat gently.

4. Put the prosciutto parcels in the grill pan and cook under the preheated grill for 2 minutes on each side, until the cheese is melting and the ham is crisp. Transfer to warmed plates and serve immediately with the sauce.

Serves 4

8 slices prosciutto
115 g/4 oz dolcelatte or Yorkshire Blue cheese, thinly sliced
4 tsp snipped fresh chives
1 pear, peeled, cored and diced
25 g/1 oz walnuts, chopped

Buttery tomato sauce
175 g/6 oz butter
2 shallots, finely chopped
1 garlic clove, finely chopped
1 celery stick, finely chopped
500 g/1 lb 2 oz plum tomatoes, peeled, cored and chopped
2 tbsp tomato purée
brown sugar, to taste
100 ml/3½ fl oz dry white wine
2 tsp snipped fresh chives
1 tbsp chopped fresh basil
salt and pepper

33

Spaghetti all'Amatriciana

1. First, make the sauce. Melt the butter with the oil in a saucepan. Add the onion, garlic, celery and carrot and cook over a low heat, stirring occasionally, for 5 minutes, until softened. Add the pancetta and cook, stirring frequently, for a further 4 minutes. Pour in the wine and cook until the alcohol has evaporated. Stir in the tomatoes, tomato purée, sugar to taste and oregano and season to taste with salt and pepper. Increase the heat to medium and bring to the boil, then reduce the heat and simmer, stirring occasionally, for 15–20 minutes, until thickened.

2. Meanwhile, bring a large pan of lightly salted water to the boil. Add the spaghetti, bring back to the boil and cook for 8–10 minutes, until tender but still firm to the bite. Drain and tip into a warmed serving dish.

3. Add the sauce to the spaghetti and toss well to coat. Sprinkle with the cheese, garnish with basil and serve immediately.

Serves 4–6

500 g/1 lb 2 oz dried spaghetti

115 g/4 oz pecorino cheese, grated

salt

chopped fresh basil, to garnish

Amatriciana sauce
* 25 g/1 oz butter
* 2 tbsp olive oil
* 1 large onion, finely chopped
* 2 garlic cloves, finely chopped
* 1 celery stick, finely chopped

1 carrot, finely chopped

175 g/6 oz pancetta or bacon, diced

100 ml/3½ fl oz dry white wine

* 400 g/14 oz canned chopped tomatoes
* 2 tbsp tomato purée
* brown sugar, to taste
* ½ tsp dried oregano
* salt and pepper

34

One-pot Lamb in Rich Red Sauce

① Cook the lamb cutlets in a large frying pan without any added fat over a medium heat for 2–3 minutes on each side, until lightly browned. Remove the pan from the heat and transfer the cutlets to a plate.

② Wipe out the pan with kitchen paper and return to the heat. Melt the butter with the oil in the pan. Add the onion, garlic, celery and peppers and cook over a low heat, stirring occasionally, for 5 minutes, until softened. Stir in the tomatoes, tomato purée, sugar to taste, basil and water and season to taste with salt and pepper. Increase the heat to medium and bring to the boil.

③ Return the cutlets to the pan, spooning the sauce over them. Reduce the heat and simmer, stirring occasionally, for 15–20 minutes, until the sauce has thickened and the lamb is tender. Stir in the olives, then taste and adjust the seasoning, adding salt and pepper if needed. Garnish with basil and serve immediately.

Serves 4

12 lamb cutlets, trimmed of excess fat
* 25 g/1 oz butter
* 2 tbsp olive oil
* 1 onion, finely chopped
* 2 garlic cloves, finely chopped
* 1 celery stick, finely chopped
  2 red peppers, deseeded and sliced
* 400 g/14 oz canned chopped tomatoes
* 2 tbsp tomato purée
* brown sugar, to taste
* 2 tbsp chopped fresh basil, plus extra to garnish
* 100 ml/3½ fl oz water
  2 tbsp chopped stoned black olives
* salt and pepper

Fried Chicken with Tomato & Bacon Sauce

First, make the sauce. Melt the butter with the oil in a large saucepan. Add the onion, garlic, celery and bacon and cook over a low heat, stirring occasionally, for 5 minutes, until softened. Stir in the tomatoes, tomato purée, sugar to taste and water and season to taste with salt and pepper. Increase the heat to medium and bring to the boil, then reduce the heat and simmer, stirring occasionally, for 15–20 minutes, until thickened.

Meanwhile, melt the butter with the oil in a large frying pan. Add the chicken and cook over a medium–high heat for 4–5 minutes on each side, until evenly browned.

Stir the basil and parsley into the sauce. Add the chicken and spoon the sauce over it. Cover and simmer for 10–15 minutes, until cooked through and tender. Garnish with parsley and serve immediately.

Serves 4

25 g/1 oz butter

2 tbsp olive oil

4 skinless, boneless chicken breasts or 8 skinless, boneless chicken thighs

Tomato & bacon sauce
* 25 g/1 oz butter
* 2 tbsp olive oil
* 1 large onion, finely chopped
* 2 garlic cloves, finely chopped
* 1 celery stick, finely chopped
  4 rashers bacon, diced
* 400 g/14 oz canned chopped tomatoes
* 2 tbsp tomato purée
* brown sugar, to taste
* 100 ml/3½ fl oz water
* 1 tbsp chopped fresh basil
* 1 tbsp chopped fresh parsley, plus extra to garnish
* salt and pepper

36

Chicken with Tomato Sauce & Melted Mozzarella

1. First, make the sauce. Melt the butter with the oil in a saucepan. Add the onion, garlic and celery and cook over a low heat, stirring occasionally, for 5 minutes, until softened. Stir in the tomatoes, tomato purée, sugar to taste, oregano and water and season to taste with salt and pepper. Increase the heat to medium and bring to the boil, then reduce the heat and simmer, stirring occasionally, for 15–20 minutes, until thickened.

2. Meanwhile, fry the bacon without any additional fat in a large frying pan over a medium heat for 5 minutes. Remove with tongs and drain on kitchen paper. Add the butter to the pan and, when it has melted, stir in the tarragon, add the chicken and cook, turning occasionally, for 15–20 minutes, until cooked through and tender.

3. Preheat the grill. Transfer the chicken to an ovenproof dish and put a bacon rasher on top of each fillet. Pour the sauce over them, cover with the mozzarella slices and cook under the preheated grill for 4–5 minutes, until the cheese has melted and is lightly browned. Serve immediately.

Serves 6

6 rashers bacon

25 g/1 oz butter

2 tsp chopped fresh tarragon

6 skinless, boneless chicken breasts, about 175 g/ 6 oz each

115 g/4 oz mozzarella cheese, sliced

Tomato sauce

* 25 g/1 oz butter
* 2 tbsp olive oil
* 1 onion, finely chopped
* 2 garlic cloves, finely chopped
* 1 celery stick, finely chopped
* 400 g/14 oz canned chopped tomatoes
* 2 tbsp tomato purée
* brown sugar, to taste
* 1 tsp dried oregano
* 100 ml/3½ fl oz water
* salt and pepper

37

Salmon & Potatoes with Tomato Sauce Topping

1. First, make the sauce. Melt the butter with the oil in a saucepan. Add the onions, garlic and celery and cook over a low heat, stirring occasionally, for 5 minutes, until softened. Stir in the tomatoes, tomato purée, sugar to taste, marjoram and wine and season to taste with salt and pepper. Increase the heat to medium and bring to the boil, then reduce the heat and simmer, stirring occasionally, for 15–20 minutes, until thickened.

2. Meanwhile, preheat the oven to 200°C/400°F/Gas Mark 6. Brush an ovenproof dish with oil. Cook the potatoes in a pan of salted boiling water for 15–20 minutes, until tender but not falling apart. Drain well and cut into thick slices. Gently toss the slices in the oil and put them around the sides of the prepared dish. Put the fish in the centre.

3. Spoon half the sauce evenly over the fish. Stir the breadcrumbs and cheese into the remainder and spoon it over the fish. Bake in the preheated oven for 15–20 minutes, until the fish flakes easily. Garnish with parsley and serve immediately.

Serves 4

12 new potatoes

1 tbsp olive oil, plus extra for brushing

4 salmon fillets

85 g/3 oz fresh breadcrumbs

55 g/2 oz Parmesan cheese, grated

salt

chopped fresh flat-leaf parsley, to garnish

Tomato sauce

* 25 g/1 oz butter
* 2 tbsp olive oil
* 2 onions, finely chopped
* 2 garlic cloves, finely chopped
* 1 celery stick, finely chopped
* 400 g/14 oz canned chopped tomatoes
* 2 tbsp tomato purée
* brown sugar, to taste
* 1 tbsp chopped fresh marjoram
  100 ml/3½ fl oz dry white wine
* salt and pepper

Monkfish with Tomato, Olive & Caper Sauce

1. First, make the sauce. Melt the butter with the oil in a saucepan. Add the shallots, garlic and celery and cook over a low heat, stirring occasionally, for 5 minutes, until softened. Stir in the tomatoes, sun-dried tomato paste, sugar to taste, capers, olives and Pernod and season to taste with salt and pepper. Increase the heat to medium and bring to the boil, then reduce the heat and simmer, stirring occasionally, for 20–25 minutes, until thickened.

2. Meanwhile, put the fish in a large pan in a single layer. Pour in the wine, add the orange rind, peppercorns and bay leaf and bring just to the boil over a medium heat. Reduce the heat so that the water is barely bubbling, cover and poach for 10–15 minutes, until the flesh flakes easily.

3. Using a fish slice, transfer the fish to a warmed serving dish. Strain the cooking liquid into the sauce and bring to the boil. Boil, stirring constantly, for 2–3 minutes, until reduced. Pour the sauce over the fish and serve immediately.

Serves 4

4 monkfish fillets, about 225 g/8 oz each
150 ml/5 fl oz dry white wine
thinly pared strip of orange rind
6 black peppercorns
1 bay leaf

Tomato, olive & caper sauce
* 25 g/1 oz butter
* 2 tbsp olive oil
2 shallots, finely chopped
* 2 garlic cloves, finely chopped
* 1 celery stick, finely chopped
* 500 g/1 lb 2 oz plum tomatoes, peeled, cored and chopped
2 tbsp sun-dried tomato paste
* brown sugar, to taste
1 tbsp capers, rinsed
55 g/2 oz black olives, stoned
1 tbsp Pernod
* salt and pepper

Baked Gnocchi with Tomato Sauce

1. To make the gnocchi, whisk the egg yolks with the granulated sugar in a saucepan until pale and creamy. Sift the flour, cornflour and salt into a bowl, then gradually beat into the egg yolk mixture. Stir in the melted butter and 85 g/3 oz of the Parmesan. Set the pan over a medium heat and gradually stir in the milk. Cook, stirring constantly, for 3–4 minutes, until thick and smooth. Remove the pan from the heat and turn out the mixture onto a baking sheet rinsed with cold water. Spread out to a thickness of 1 cm/½ inch and smooth the surface. Chill in the refrigerator for 30 minutes.

2. Meanwhile, make the sauce. Melt the butter with the oil in a saucepan. Add the onion, garlic and celery and cook over a low heat, stirring occasionally, for 5 minutes, until softened. Stir in the tomatoes, tomato purée, brown sugar to taste, vermouth, parsley and water and season to taste with salt and pepper. Increase the heat to medium and bring to the boil, then reduce the heat and simmer, stirring occasionally, for 25–30 minutes, until thickened.

3. Preheat the oven to 190°C/375°F/Gas Mark 5. Grease an ovenproof dish with butter. Cut the gnocchi into 3–4-cm/1¼–1½-inch squares and put them into the prepared dish, slightly overlapping. Bake in the preheated oven for 15 minutes. Pour the tomato sauce over the top and bake for a further 5–10 minutes, until hot. Sprinkle with the remaining Parmesan, garnish with parsley and serve immediately.

Serves 4

4 egg yolks
2 tsp granulated sugar
55 g/2 oz plain flour
2 tbsp cornflour
pinch of salt
55 g/2 oz butter, melted, plus extra for greasing
115 g/4 oz Parmesan cheese, grated
425 ml/15 fl oz milk

Tomato sauce
* 25 g/1 oz butter
* 2 tbsp olive oil
* 1 onion, finely chopped
* 2 garlic cloves, finely chopped
* 1 celery stick, finely chopped
* 800 g/1 lb 12 oz canned chopped tomatoes
* 2 tbsp tomato purée
* brown sugar, to taste
* 1 tbsp dry vermouth
* 1 tbsp chopped fresh flat-leaf parsley, plus extra to garnish
* 5 tbsp water
* salt and pepper

40

Spinach Crêpes with Tomato Sauce

1. To make the crêpe batter, sift the flour and salt into a bowl and make a well in the centre. Add the eggs and melted butter and mix together, gradually incorporating the dry ingredients. Mix the milk and water in a jug and gradually beat into the mixture to form a smooth batter.

2. Cook the spinach, in just the water clinging to the leaves after washing, for 5–10 minutes, until wilted. Drain well, pressing out as much liquid as possible. Transfer to a food processor or blender and process to a purée. Stir the spinach into the batter, cover with clingfilm and leave to rest in a cool place.

3. Meanwhile, pour the tomato sauce into a large saucepan and place over a low heat. Heat gently until warmed through.

4. Stir the batter. Heat a 20-cm/8-inch frying pan over a medium heat and brush with a little melted butter. Pour 3–4 tablespoons of the batter into the pan, then tilt and rotate the pan to spread the batter evenly over the base. Cook for 30–45 seconds, until the crêpe is set and the underside is golden. Shake the pan to loosen the crêpe, then flip over with a palette knife and cook the other side for 30 seconds. Slide onto a plate. Cook more crêpes in the same way, stacking them interleaved with greaseproof paper.

5. Roll up or fold the crêpes and put them on a serving dish. Spoon the tomato sauce over them and serve immediately.

Serves 4–6

225 g/8 oz plain flour

pinch of salt

4 eggs

4 tbsp melted butter, plus extra for brushing

225 ml/8 fl oz milk

200 ml/7 fl oz water

500 g/1 lb 2 oz spinach, coarse stalks removed

* 1 quantity Basic Tomato Sauce (see page 8)

Special

41

Steak Pizzaiola

1. First, make the sauce. Melt the butter with the oil in a saucepan. Add the onion and garlic and cook over a low heat, stirring occasionally, for 5 minutes, until softened. Stir in the tomatoes, tomato purée, sugar to taste, olives, basil, oregano and water and season to taste with salt and pepper. Increase the heat to medium and bring to the boil, then reduce the heat and simmer, stirring occasionally, for 15–20 minutes, until thickened.

2. Heat the oil in a large frying pan. Add the steaks and cook over a medium heat for 2–3 minutes on each side. Spoon the sauce over each steak and cook for a further 5 minutes. Serve immediately.

Serves 4

3 tbsp olive oil

4 porterhouse steaks, about 225 g/8 oz each

Pizzaiola sauce
* 25 g/1 oz butter
* 2 tbsp olive oil
* 1 onion, finely chopped
* 2 garlic cloves, finely chopped
* 500 g/1 lb 2 oz plum tomatoes, peeled, cored and chopped
* 2 tbsp tomato purée
* brown sugar, to taste
* 115 g/4 oz green olives, stoned and quartered
* 1 tbsp chopped fresh basil
* 1 tsp dried oregano
* 100 ml/3½ fl oz water
* salt and pepper

42

Pork Chops with Creamy Tomato Sauce

1. Preheat the oven to 180°C/350°F/Gas Mark 4. Rub the chops all over with salt, pepper and two thirds of the garlic. Melt the butter with the oil in a large flameproof casserole. Add the chops and cook over a medium heat for 3–4 minutes on each side, until lightly browned. Remove from the casserole and keep warm.

2. Add the shallots, the remaining garlic and the celery to the casserole, reduce the heat and cook, stirring occasionally, for 5 minutes, until softened. Stir in the tomatoes, tomato purée and sugar to taste and cook, stirring frequently, for 5 minutes. Stir in the mushrooms and sage, season to taste with salt and pepper and cook, stirring frequently, for a further 5 minutes.

3. Return the chops to the casserole and pour in the wine and stock. Cover, transfer to the preheated oven and bake for 30 minutes. Remove the lid, return the casserole to the oven and bake for a further 15 minutes, until the meat is tender and cooked through.

4. Transfer the chops to a warmed serving dish and keep warm. Bring the sauce to the boil over a medium–high heat and boil for 5–8 minutes, until reduced by half. Remove the casserole from the heat and stir in the cream. Pour the sauce over the chops, garnish with sage and serve immediately.

Serves 4

4 pork chops
* 3 garlic cloves, finely chopped
* 25 g/1 oz butter
* 2 tbsp olive oil
2 shallots, finely chopped
* 1 celery stick, finely chopped
* 500 g/1 lb 2 oz plum tomatoes, peeled, cored and chopped
* 2 tbsp tomato purée
* brown sugar, to taste
225 g/8 oz button mushrooms, thinly sliced
* 1 tbsp chopped fresh sage, plus extra to garnish
50 ml/2 fl oz white wine
50 ml/2 fl oz chicken stock
50 ml/2 fl oz double cream
* salt and pepper

43

Lamb Chops in Tomato Sauce with Broad Beans

1. Season the chops with salt and pepper to taste. Melt the butter with the oil in a large frying pan. Add the chops and cook over a medium heat for 1–1½ minutes on each side, until evenly browned. Remove the chops from the pan and set aside.

2. Add the onion, garlic, celery and pancetta to the pan and cook over a low heat, stirring occasionally, for 5 minutes, until the onion has softened. Stir in the tomatoes, tomato purée, sugar to taste, basil, vinegar and water and season to taste with salt and pepper. Increase the heat to medium and bring to the boil, then reduce the heat and simmer, stirring occasionally, for 10 minutes.

3. Return the chops to the pan and add the broad beans. Partially cover and simmer for 10 minutes, until the lamb is tender and cooked through. Transfer to a warmed serving dish and serve immediately.

Serves 4

- 8 lamb chops
- 25 g/1 oz butter
- 2 tbsp olive oil
- 1 onion, finely chopped
- 2 garlic cloves, finely chopped
- 1 celery stick, finely chopped
- 40 g/1½ oz pancetta or bacon, diced
- 400 g/14 oz canned chopped tomatoes
- 2 tbsp tomato purée
- brown sugar, to taste
- 2 tbsp chopped fresh basil
- 1 tbsp red wine vinegar
- 100 ml/3½ fl oz water
- 350 g/12 oz shelled fresh or frozen broad beans, grey skins removed
- salt and pepper

44

Spanish Chicken with Tomato & Chocolate Sauce

① Dust the chicken portions with flour. Heat the oil in a large frying pan. Add the chicken, in batches if necessary, and cook over a medium heat, turning occasionally, for 8–10 minutes, until evenly browned. Remove the chicken from the pan and drain on kitchen paper.

② Drain off the fat from the pan and wipe out with kitchen paper. To make the sauce, melt the butter with the oil in the same pan. Add the onion, garlic and red pepper and cook over a low heat, stirring occasionally, for 5 minutes, until softened. Stir in the tomatoes, tomato purée, sugar to taste, nutmeg, cinnamon, cloves and wine and season to taste with salt and pepper. Increase the heat to medium and bring to the boil.

③ Return the chicken to the pan, reduce the heat, cover and simmer for 20 minutes. Remove the lid from the pan and simmer for a further 20 minutes, until the chicken is cooked through and tender and the sauce has thickened. Add the chopped chocolate and stir constantly until it has melted. Garnish with grated chocolate and serve immediately.

Serves 6

6 chicken portions

plain flour, for dusting

4 tbsp olive oil

Tomato & chocolate sauce

✳ 25 g/1 oz butter

✳ 2 tbsp olive oil

✳ 1 onion, finely chopped

✳ 2 garlic cloves, finely chopped

1 red pepper, deseeded and sliced

✳ 800 g/1 lb 12 oz canned chopped tomatoes

✳ 2 tbsp tomato purée

✳ brown sugar, to taste

½ tsp ground nutmeg

½ tsp ground cinnamon

¼ tsp ground cloves

250 ml/9 fl oz dry white wine

70 g/2½ oz dark chocolate, finely chopped, plus extra grated chocolate to garnish

✳ salt and pepper

Duck with Tomato & Orange Sauce

1. First, make the sauce. Melt the butter with the oil in a saucepan. Add the shallots, garlic and celery and cook over a low heat, stirring occasionally, for 5 minutes, until softened. Stir in the tomatoes, tomato purée, sugar, stock, orange juice, wine and vinegar and season to taste with salt and pepper. Increase the heat to medium and bring to the boil, then reduce the heat and simmer, stirring occasionally, for 20–30 minutes, until thickened.

2. Heat a griddle pan. Score the skin of the duck breasts through to the flesh. When the griddle pan is hot, add the duck breasts, skin-side down, and cook for 8–10 minutes. Turn them over and cook for a further 4–6 minutes on the other side.

3. Meanwhile, remove the pan of sauce from the heat and leave to cool slightly. Ladle it into a food processor or blender and process to a purée. Pass the purée through a sieve into a clean pan and heat through gently. If you prefer a thicker sauce, bring to the boil and boil, stirring constantly, until reduced.

4. Divide the sauce among four warmed individual plates. Top each with a duck breast, garnish with basil leaves and serve immediately.

Serves 4

4 Barbary duck breasts
fresh basil leaves, to garnish

Tomato & orange sauce
* 25 g/1 oz butter
* 2 tbsp olive oil
  2 shallots, finely chopped
* 1 garlic clove, finely chopped
* 1 celery stick, finely chopped
* 500 g/1 lb 2 oz plum tomatoes, peeled, cored and chopped
* 2 tbsp tomato purée
* 1 tsp brown sugar
  3 tbsp chicken stock
  juice of 2 oranges
  2 tbsp dry white wine
  1 tsp white wine vinegar
* salt and pepper

46

Halibut in Tomato & Wine Sauce

1. Mix together the flour, coriander, oregano and ½ teaspoon each of salt and pepper in a shallow dish. Coat the fish fillets in the seasoned flour, shaking off the excess. Melt the butter with the oil in a large frying pan. Add the fish and cook over a medium heat for 5 minutes on each side, until evenly browned. Remove with a fish slice and keep warm.

2. Add the shallots, garlic and celery to the pan, reduce the heat to low and cook, stirring occasionally, for 5 minutes, until softened. Stir in the tomatoes, tomato purée, sugar to taste, bay leaf, wine and vinegar and season to taste with salt and pepper. Increase the heat to medium and bring to the boil. Return the fish to the pan and add the prawns. Reduce the heat, cover and simmer for 20 minutes, until the fish flakes easily.

3. Transfer the halibut and prawns to a warmed serving dish and keep warm. Increase the heat to high and bring the sauce to the boil, stirring constantly. Cook, stirring frequently, for 3–4 minutes, until reduced and thickened. Remove and discard the bay leaf and pour the sauce over the fish and prawns. Serve immediately.

Serves 4

- 4 tbsp plain flour
- 1 tbsp finely chopped fresh coriander
- ½ tsp dried oregano
- 4 halibut fillets, about 175 g/6 oz each
- 25 g/1 oz butter
- 2 tbsp olive oil
- 2 shallots, finely chopped
- 1 garlic clove, finely chopped
- 1 celery stick, finely chopped
- 1 kg/2 lb 4 oz plum tomatoes, peeled, deseeded and chopped
- 2 tbsp tomato purée
- brown sugar, to taste
- 1 bay leaf
- 300 ml/10 fl oz dry white wine
- 2 tbsp tarragon vinegar
- 225 g/8 oz raw prawns, peeled and deveined
- salt and pepper

47

Mussels Baked in Tomato & Basil Sauce

1. Scrub the mussels under cold running water and pull off the beards. Discard any with broken shells and any that refuse to close when tapped. Put the lemon slices in a heavy saucepan, add the mussels and pour in the wine. Cover and cook over a high heat, shaking the pan occasionally, for 4–6 minutes, until the shells have opened. Remove with a slotted spoon and discard any mussels that remain closed. Strain the cooking liquid through a muslin-lined strainer into a bowl.

2. To make the sauce, melt the butter with the oil in a saucepan. Add the shallots, garlic and celery and cook over a low heat, stirring occasionally, for 5 minutes, until softened. Stir in the tomatoes, tomato purée, sugar to taste, basil, bay leaf and the reserved cooking liquid and season to taste with salt and pepper. Increase the heat to medium and bring to the boil, then reduce the heat and simmer, stirring occasionally, for 15 minutes.

3. Meanwhile, preheat the oven to 180°C/350°F/Gas Mark 4. Grease an ovenproof dish with butter. Remove the mussels from their shells. Mix together the breadcrumbs and cheese.

4. Remove and discard the bay leaf from the sauce and gently stir in the mussels. Pour the mixture into the prepared dish, sprinkle with the breadcrumb mixture and bake in the preheated oven for 20 minutes, until the topping is golden and bubbling. Serve immediately.

Serves 4

2 kg/4 lb 8 oz live mussels
1 lemon, sliced
150 ml/5 fl oz dry white wine
butter, for greasing
2 tbsp fresh breadcrumbs
55 g/2 oz Parmesan cheese, grated

Tomato & basil sauce
25 g/1 oz butter
2 tbsp olive oil
4 shallots, finely chopped
3 garlic cloves, finely chopped
2 celery sticks, finely chopped
600 g/1 lb 5 oz canned chopped tomatoes
2 tbsp tomato purée
brown sugar, to taste
3 tbsp chopped fresh basil
1 bay leaf
salt and pepper

48

Scallops in Tomato Sauce

1. First, make the sauce. Melt the butter with the oil in a saucepan. Add the shallots and whole garlic clove and cook over a low heat, stirring occasionally, for 5 minutes, until softened. Stir in the tomatoes, tomato purée, sugar to taste, dill, parsley, mint and water and season to taste with salt and pepper. Increase the heat to medium and bring to the boil, then reduce the heat and simmer, stirring occasionally, for 15–20 minutes, until thickened.

2. Heat the oil with the sea salt in a non-stick or heavy-based frying pan. Add the scallops and cook for 2 minutes on each side, until golden. Remove from the pan and transfer to a serving dish.

3. Remove and discard the garlic from the sauce and spoon the sauce over the scallops. Garnish with dill and serve immediately.

Serves 4–6

2 tbsp olive oil
1 tbsp coarse sea salt
24 scallops, shelled

Tomato sauce
- 25 g/1 oz butter
- 2 tbsp olive oil
- 2 shallots, finely chopped
- 1 garlic clove, peeled
- 500 g/1 lb 2 oz plum tomatoes, peeled, cored and chopped
- 2 tbsp tomato purée
- brown sugar, to taste
- 2 tbsp chopped fresh dill, plus extra to garnish
- 2 tbsp chopped fresh parsley
- 1 tbsp chopped fresh mint
- 100 ml/3½ fl oz water
- salt and pepper

Slow-cooked Potato Stew

① Parboil the potatoes in a saucepan of salted boiling water for 5 minutes. Drain and set aside.

② Melt the butter with the oil in a saucepan. Add the pancetta, onion, garlic and celery and cook over a low heat, stirring occasionally, for 5 minutes, until softened. Stir in the tomatoes, tomato purée, sugar to taste, marjoram and stock and season to taste with salt and pepper. Increase the heat to medium and bring to the boil. Gently stir in the potatoes, reduce the heat to very low, cover and simmer, stirring occasionally, for 45–50 minutes, until the potatoes are tender and the sauce has thickened. (Use a fork to stir gently to avoid breaking up the potatoes.)

③ Taste and adjust the seasoning, adding salt and pepper if needed. Transfer the mixture to a warmed serving dish and serve immediately.

Serves 4

700 g/1 lb 9 oz waxy potatoes, cut into 2.5-cm/1-inch cubes

✳ 25 g/1 oz butter

✳ 2 tbsp olive oil

55 g/2 oz pancetta or bacon, diced

✳ 1 onion, finely chopped

✳ 1 garlic clove, finely chopped

✳ 1 celery stick, finely chopped

✳ 400 g/14 oz canned chopped tomatoes

✳ 2 tbsp tomato purée

✳ brown sugar, to taste

✳ 1 tbsp chopped fresh marjoram

100 ml/3½ fl oz vegetable stock

✳ salt and pepper

Polenta, Cheese & Tomato Sauce Gratin

1. Line a 28 x 18-cm/11 x 7-inch cake tin with clingfilm. Pour the 1 litre/1¾ pints of water into a large saucepan and bring to the boil. Stir the salt into the water. While stirring constantly, pour the polenta into the pan in a steady stream, then cook, stirring constantly, for 5 minutes. Stir in the mace and paprika, then pour the mixture into the prepared tin. Smooth the surface and leave to cool.

2. To make the sauce, melt the butter with the oil in a saucepan. Add the onion, garlic and celery and cook over a low heat, stirring occasionally, for 5 minutes, until softened. Stir in the tomatoes, tomato purée, sugar to taste, parsley and water and season to taste with salt and pepper. Increase the heat to medium and bring to the boil, then reduce the heat and simmer, stirring occasionally, for 15–20 minutes, until thickened.

3. Meanwhile, preheat the oven to 200°C/400°F/Gas Mark 6. Grease an ovenproof dish with butter.

4. Turn out the polenta onto a chopping board and cut into 2.5-cm/1-inch squares. Remove the sauce from the heat. Put half the polenta squares into the prepared dish and spoon half the sauce over them, then sprinkle with half the cheese. Repeat the layers. Bake in the preheated oven for 30 minutes, until the topping is golden brown and bubbling. Serve immediately.

Serves 4

1 litre/1¾ pints water
1 tsp salt
250 g/9 oz quick-cook polenta
pinch of ground mace
1 tsp paprika
butter, for greasing
85 g/3 oz Gruyère or
 Emmenthal cheese, grated

Tomato sauce

* 25 g/1 oz butter
* 2 tbsp olive oil
* 1 Spanish onion,
 finely chopped
* 2 garlic cloves, finely chopped
* 1 celery stick, finely chopped
* 800 g/1 lb 12 oz canned
 chopped tomatoes
* 2 tbsp tomato purée
* brown sugar, to taste
* 1 tbsp chopped fresh flat-leaf
 parsley
* 100 ml/3½ fl oz water
* salt and pepper